PURGINGS

By

Georgia Caldwell

I wonder where this writing will go
these words I can't seem to stop the flow
one two maybe three
writing is overtaking me
daily thoughts go through my mind
pen and paper I hurry to find
Words flowing smooth like streams
when I'm awake and asleep in my dreams
Loops and lines I frantically make
I's dotted t's crossed hurry the momentum is at stake
attempts to make my words rhyme and mix
just like a feign on the hunt for a fix
wanting to capture every thought
self-expression is what this has brought
an outlet for joy hurt and pain
and anything else that might remain
like the freedom I feel with the breeze on my face
or the need to have my space
maybe I will write about my past present and future
or these babies I am trying to nurture
I could certainly write about my God how amazing
or the love I seem to be chasing
its liberating to be able to say what I feel
Actually surreal

Childhood

Fairytale Day Dreams

Always been a part of me it seems
Since my youth
Always dreaming little detached from the truth
Gazing at the sunset and all its glory
Praying for another life story
I wonder how many years
When did my eyes begin filling with tears
While my heart dreamed
The Creator didn't hear me it seemed
Dreams of being an artist filled my mind
Drawing and sketching searching to find
Someway to be good enough
Instead spirit broken exterior rough
Dreams seemed to disappear
Smoking and survival now my atmosphere
Fairytale dreams just weren't for me
Just look at my past you will agree
Lost dreams, broken trust, abandonment
Rejection, failure, mental entrapment
But still a spark of hope
I could still see the stars no telescope
I started to find my dreams one by one
The Creator showed the way and gave light like the sun
I am finding my dreams and more
Some have come to pass and more is in store
I feel like I'm on a new adventure
Each day something new and old to recapture
Its true what's for me is for me
No one can steal my dreams keeping hope that is key

Wounded Heart

A wounded heart
How does it happen when did it start
To no longer trust and to fear
To be so sensitive have so many tears
To hurt so bad there is an aching deep in my chest
I try to be strong I give it my best
But my heart seems to be the dictator
Past wounds the instigator
Sometimes I wish I could hide
Keep it controlled bottled inside
My eyes give it away
No matter the time of the day
Maybe some sunglasses and a mask
They would cover up they would do the task
There are times I need my heart to show
I need people to believe me I want them to know
That I am genuine and they can trust
I realize now I have to do the same I must
This is when fear steps in
Walls come up and I start to examine
Reasons why they can't love me
Predicting things I really can't foresee
Hypervigilance skews my perception
Wanting to guard my heart from all deception
Childhood lies I was told
Now deeply rooted they take hold
Fear of abandonment and rejection
A continuous longing for deep connection
Bars of survival is what's keeping me
Facing my fears is the key
If I stay still and don't flee
Maybe I will get the healing that will set me free

Hiding

So many years of hiding
Behind chaos that was blinding
Behind my own protective shell
That in time would turn to a living hell
Keep a safe distance no obligation
Trapped in my own isolation
Protecting myself from the harm that had been done
Never to experience again on the run
I didn't know what to do
Telling myself the only one that will protect you is you
So I did the best I knew how
It worked for then but not now
Memories and pain buried deep
Many nights just couldn't sleep
Defenses and self-protection was how I would live
Unable to see how my survival didn't allow me to give
Or receive the love I wanted
Unknowingly repeating patterns of my past haunted
Could I break this cycle of keeping people out?
Glimpses of my reality making me want to shout
I could not control what life would deal
So I had to look back I had to heal
No longer can I live this way
I can't hide I can't betray
Cause really it's myself I'm losing
Trying something different is what I am choosing
Today learning to be ok with uncomfortable
Learning how to be open and vulnerable
No longer pretending or hiding who I am created to be
Accepting and loving all of me

Survival

Surviving started at an early age
I could perform on almost any stage
Masks I learn to use
Never knowing it was me I would lose
Wanting to fit and belong
Truth is I never felt good enough all along
My imperfections is all I could see
More shortcomings is all they would tell me
So I tried to become something they would want
My inability to do this seemed to haunt
Surviving left me guessing
Answers and direction always pressing
Vigilant about my surrounding
Glimpses of love left my heart pounding
Anxieties and fears left me dreaming
Curled in my bed screaming
Survival only works for so long
And I can no longer be strong
The walls I have built are falling apart
No more protecting my heart
Those that come close don't understand
They trip over my rubble looking for my hand
Either leaving over the hurt I inflicted
Or gave up because these chains had me restricted
So here I am covered with wounds and scars
Wanted desperately to be free from these bars
Survival has turned on me
Once keeping me safe now in captivity
Of these lies and delusions
Glimpses of truth causing confusions
More than anything the truth I want to be told
Purged of the beliefs breaking this mold
Living a life that is true to me
Survival no longer the way to live I see

Confusion

Mixed messages of love and hate
This is how it has always been... my fate
They say I love you as my own
But publicly disown
He says you are amazing no one is greater
I promise I will leave my wife later
She says you're my girl I got your back
When things don't go her way she talks smack
You're normal you're okay
But your too sensitive grow up he'd say
Ongoing conflicts of love and hate
I guess this is my fate
Wonder how things would have been different
If I had another upbringing other parents
One's that gazed at me with admiration
Versus emotional separation
Being cared for and soothed by a mothers song
Not pointing out all that was wrong
A father that would call me princess
Probably wouldn't struggle with feeling less
A mother that would show me how to be a lady
Probably wouldn't deal with these dudes so shady
A father that could hold me in a loving way
No more guessing who is going to stay
A mother to show me how to love my curves and hips
No more searching for validation from someone else's lips
A father who was consistent and took care of his wife
Maybe I wouldn't be doing this alone....this life
Mother who loved her man and let him do his part
Maybe I would trust with my heart
I wonder what it would have been like for you all to be
proud of me
Bragging about my gifts for the world to see
What would have it been like to have a parents approval
Maybe I wouldn't have all this shame ready for removal

Show up to my games
Have my pictures hung in frames
What would have it been like to hear an encouraging word
If my imperfections weren't all I heard
If my spirit would have been uplifted
Maybe we would have all been a bit more gifted
By real love so unconditional
I guess for our family that wasn't so traditional
But I wonder if we could have been honest with no fears
I am sure we would have shed far less tears
I just wonder what would have happened to the family
If it had been different...that just wasn't reality

Feeted Pajamas

I remember when I was little in feeted pajamas
And when it all started that 4th of July at grandmas
Insecure and unaware of my beauty and worth
Words he used to have his way and give birth
Coaxing me with words longed for
Confused and tore
The words and liquor
Repeated scars to my core
First kisses and hands on my breast
I wish that was all that was the rest
He unzipped his pants and forced my hand on his -----
I thought it was gross but couldn't speak up words on lock
He pushed my head down
I tried to resist still no words bound
Gagging and tears falling
Where was my voice no screaming or calling?
Speechless unable to fight
And I wouldn't even after this night
This is what it came down to
A continuous forfeit tried and true
Brief glimpses of fraudulous wanting
Sacrificing myself forever haunting
Years of this repetitive pattern
Until a light was shown a lantern
Feeling unworthy not good enough
Settling for physical sacrifice and a puff
Looking back on it now
Shaking my head wondering how
A beautiful talented girl
Could not see her worth...a pearl

A gem one of a kind
Woe to those who planted lies in her mind
Not telling her the truth
From the beginning in her youth
My own worth and value I am finding
Self-love now embracing and the past I am binding

Cast aside

From my birth cast aside
This pain I can no longer hide
Undeserving of this great thing called love
This is the truth I know of
Searching for acceptance and worth all my life
Internal turmoil ongoing strife
All my life feeling dispensable
My worth at times uncomprehend able
Wanting to be claimed by mom or dad
This is too much am I that bad?
My value I was not told
I have searched for its worth to me like gold
If I knew this truth and could remove this lie
My life would change no need to cry
I hear people say girl you're amazing
At your smile I could spend the day gazing
Lady you have such a gift!
Your words encourage and my spirits lift
You're a great mom you have been so strong
Taking care of your family all along
All these great things people do say
I wish I could believe them and in my head they would stay
But no doubts fears and criticism ring in my ears
I wonder if I will be free or will it go on for years
Love is what I desire
Don't let go not even through the fire
My defenses they will come down
I won't run I promise I won't skip town
Just stick with me as I go through this process
Is that too much to ask maybe so may be yes
God will you stay then
No matter how bad I have been
Will you love me no matter what?
Or will that door shut
I need someone to be here

Someone that will stay near
I promise to keep working on these defects
If you can't I understand and give you your respects
I don't want to burden or empty you
I just really don't know what to do
My mind a bit confused
And my heart jeez so easily bruised
No more dispensable like a dirty rag
A worth more valuable no dollar amount no tag
Confidence and humility a perfect mix
With broken empty things I no longer attempt to fix
So a new outlook
A new story a new book
These pieces I gather of my life in ink
Going back and making me think
I begin to write a new line a testimony
Seeing, hearing, and believing all in harmony

Truth

Hiding the truth I cannot do
The facade only elevated you
Speaking my truth now is a must
For so long I have questioned and could not trust
What I felt what I knew what was on the inside of me
Now more than ever I just long to be free
Condemnation blame is not my goal
For years I have just wanted to feel whole
Because of your own story mine you could not validate
So I'm going to do my best to keep it real and give it to you
straight
On this paper I will write
What my reality was both day and night
Answers I searched for
Met with a closed door
Feelings of hope, love, and confusion
Always an inconvenient intrusion
Yes from my birth an unwanted feeling
But you made very clear my parents weren't worth dealing
So with hate you spoke of them often
Reminding me they left me orphan
Worthless they were described to me
How could anything good come from them you see?
As a child I loved you all
I believe being full of hope has been part of my call
Your acceptance and affirmation is what I needed so to
your rule I heeded
Pushing aside my questions and fears
Praying to the sunset face filled with tears
Your approval is what I sought to get
Not quite good enough not yet
To be your daughter in private was ok
But to the rest just a stray
Not ready to claim me as your own
But as a mother you were all I had known

Loved in private but outcast in the open
Praying this pattern would break searching and hopin
But relationship after relationship it seems I
sought those out
Repeating what you taught me, I needed another route
So here I am today affirming my past reality
So I can rid myself of this false mentality
To speak truth about my story

Freedom

Trapped in a swirl of racing thought
Doubts, fears, and messages I was taught
Made to hide who I was created to be
Not ever enough for her you see
Mixed messages of love
Something it seemed I was undeserving of
My thighs to thick
These words would stick
Your art could be better
You look like a whore in that sweater
Attempts to please you
I couldn't seem too
Longing to belong
Your words hurt they were so strong
My spirit it was broke
Now words of anger I spoke
My hope
Traded for dope
To dull the pain
The only joy I would gain
For years to come I would still seek you out
In efforts to heal and find another route

Approval, belonging, and acceptance
From you I wanted even if from a distance
This hasn't been something you could offer
So I am reminded of my life you are not the author
Your lies uttered and unspoken
Will no longer leave me broken!
Because love you do not earn
This has taken me awhile to learn
My beauty cannot be hidden
And my creation was not forbidden!
My talents and abilities were gifts given
To share with the world as long as I'm livin
My abilities and frailties are what make me human
My acceptability not determined by any man or woman
Freedom is what I feel!
From the past I do heal!

Torment

This emotional torment must heed
Makes me want to cut to bleed
A concoction of negative emotion
I need something a numbing potion
The shame insecurity and rejection
Oh and did I mention
The words like daggers that cut
Your just like your mother you slut
That's what you would say
When your nephew would have his way
When your friend took my virginity
Blaming words you spit at me
Instead of wrapped in your embrace
I became the family disgrace
To this day you are poison to my being
Confusion in my heart, mind, at times I don't know what
I'm feeling
Mixing acts of love rooted in hate
Causing this confusion this can't be my fate
Repeating the cycle you taught
I see it now I can't get caught
Reversing this deception so engrained seems daunting
Progress made then words shame becomes haunting
I get confused like it's your acceptance and love I desire
Seeking out relationships like you I tire
Trying to find love
From places it's unheard of
No longer wanting to listen to your voice and what it has
to say
No longer accepting those mixes of love and hate today
Teach me Creator what true love is
How does it feel what are its messages
Make it so clear to me there is no question
Living free no more oppression

Few Chapters

So many words and ideas where to start
All significant coming from my heart
Writing about my childhood
For my soul has been so good
My hopeless romantic ways
Writing about my lover's gaze
Thoughts of my marriage and divorce
Loss and gain given another course
About the power of overcoming
To my past not succumbing
Writing about my struggle with faith and doubt
How my Creator has had His hand on me brought me out
Let me write a little more
Let's talk about all the closed and opened doors
Wild smoked out disrespectful teenager
To the streets and chaos no stranger
Independent unruly on my own
Working paying bills trying to be grown
Seventeen consoling my babies cry
I child turned to mother I would try
So many promises I made to you
Of all the things I would and wouldn't do
Smokin' drinkin' trying to find an answer
Destroying myself like cancer
Looking for love in empty arms
Wanting it so bad not seeing the alarms
Before I know it another baby on the way
I am confused I don't know what to do or say
21 yrs. old single mother of two
No smokin no drinkin my responsibilities grew
Welfare check and food stamps were humbling
It helped me though I'm not grumbling
Going to school because I had aspirations
No welfare momma for life I had a destination
Going to church and readin the word

Preaching about forgiveness and healing is what I heard
Working going to church and taking care of family
No more state support doing it independently
Money would get tight
Have me tossin and turning through the night
But bills have always been paid
Always had food and in a house always stayed
There is so much more to write
Not sure if I will get it all in tonight
There have been times of bad choices
And time of nothing but rejoices
My Creator has always been near
But I have strayed in independence and fear
Two more children would soon come along
For the road ahead I would need to be strong
A husband who struggled with his own demons
I did all I could had to leave....I had reasons
Four children now we ventured to Tennessee
The accent was strong and everyone called me sweetie
The children adapted okay
Uprooted from their home but in Tennessee we would
stay
New schools new friends and new home
I tried to make it fun so we would roam
Downtown, Radnor Lake, and Centennial Park
New life new adventures we would embark
Memories of what we left I try to forget
Attempts to move forward with no regrets
Still the past haunts me now
A ripple effect of my choices wish I could fix somehow
My Creator continues to protect and provide
I know He is with me right alongside
Helping me with my family
Giving us a life where we can live happily
My life has been a bit of a roller coaster

And where I am today I cannot boaster
Because despite my losses and history
He didn't have to do it open all these doors for me
I have made a lot of bad calls
Gotten some bruises had a lot of falls
But my God is always right there
Sometimes with a hand and sometimes with an
encouraging stare
His faith in me is great
I don't know what it is but He sees my fate
I am thankful for my life's story
And any good He gets the glory!

The rain always stops…….

Balance

Everyday something new
I wonder if balance is something I can do
A life of turbulence and ordered chaos
Without it I'm at a loss
Untamed in my spirit body mind and heart
Gets unmanageable and I don't know where to start
Daily prayer and meditation is great
But I want more.... to over flow with His presence and to
know my fate
Money comes and quickly goes
Either broke or just enough to do my toes
I want to find some middle ground
I know the steps but I feel bound
I do it for a little while and get off track
Eating exercise journaling too...the discipline feels whack!
Funny but serious too
For so long I just did what I do
If I started to feel trapped or not in control
Good bye see ya and off I would stroll
Self-control and discipline I feels to confined
And if I stuck with it I wouldn't mind
But no this energy comes over me
Filled with ideas and urgency
There is something wild and untamed inside
Failed attempts to control I've tried
So much I feel like I'm coming out of my skin
Searching and looking for ways to give in
Feeling overpowered and defeated by my lack of discipline
Every day like the Phoenix a new beginnin
Wish I had that power and freedom
I would fly away to another kingdom
No restraints of responsibility or time
Oh the depths and heights I would climb
....how quick my daydreams vanish
Oh reality if your restraints I could banish

Refrain

Refraining from this emotional ride
Trying to take each second in stride
I get my footing about me
swirls by again no cost it's free
Ride of adrenaline mixed with shame hurt and rage
Tornado of emotions locked in like a cage
It's a cocktail of abandonment pain and loss
I get drunk completely wasted curled in my bed I toss
Each passenger screams for me to come along
Feeling weak and need to be strong
My own emotions have betrayed me
Preying on my wounds and patterns see
Showing me faulty facts
Convincing arguments for my acts
But as I hold them up they reflect
Cracks and defect
Betrayed by my own emotions
They lie to me causing chaos and commotions
When did this start?
So much power over my mind and heart...
Suffocating my life and relationships
Just a host for you to breed your madness grips
Disguising lies as truth
Twisting facts ignoring the proof
Until today a brief glimpse of the clarity
Hope.... no longer have to choose emotional disparity

Numb

My body is numb
My hands my lips
My hearts not heavy
But there is a little sickness I feel In the pit of my stomach
Life is good I mean real good
But I feel like escaping
Vanishing In the clouds
Melting in the rain drops
Slowly gracefully taken with the wind
Or consumed by the earth
No particular thing has occurred
But I feel the frustration of something
It's pushing on the forefront of my skull
As I attempt to walk this out
The air breathes on my face
The clouds of the storm begin to cover me
While the night comes
Lingering piercing through is the sunset and what's left of
the blue sky
The rain is coming
It's trapped in the atmosphere but u can feel it
You can smell it
My tears are trapped
They usually flow so naturally
So easily
But not today I can feel them like the rain in the
atmosphere
And like the rain and storm they will come
Like the rain and storm they come to an end
The sky will be bluer the grass greener and the air fresher

Junkie

Emotional junkie
Healthy relationship flunky
Grasping on to those in need
Really because of my own greed
Always over the top
Not sure how to stop
Joy junkie feel good feign
It's ok not all will know what I mean
Feel feel feel I can't get enough
Gets me high like fluff
Unstoppable over flowing excitement
Briefly all will crash and you wonder where it went
No more joy only sorrow
No more hope darkness fills my tomorrow
Feeling alone and misunderstood
A break from this life I wish I could
Confused and full of fears
Face filled with smiles now with tears
A roller coaster ride of emotions
I can't stop the high or drop no precautions
Just sit back and go for the ride
With this pen on this paper confide
The adrenaline that comes with the highs
The darkness in the drop that waits and lies

Fucking issues

Tired of the failed attempts used up tissues
Trying to hold it together
Damn it why can't I just do this forever
Sustain the unsustainable
Other people do it why am I incapable
Self-discipline and consistency
Uncontrolled and complacency
More lack of focus and impulsivity
I feel like a fuckin calamity
I want to curl in my bed
Pulls the covers over my head
Let this fear and anxiety out
Praying God show me another route
I just can't do this on my own
Feel like I should shit I'm grown
Asking God take away my crutch
Which one? You have so much!
Every last one
I want to be done
Just face things as the come
Be able to deal all the time just not some
Tired of falling apart
Tired of the restart
Don't get me wrong
Thankful and I get up try to be strong
Get so mad at myself for the chaos and trouble
Mostly self-inflicted so I can't grumble
So I'm prayin for the strength
For the endurance to go any length
To make those painful changes
Destruction for life exchanges

Fear

I would be lying if I denied
How this fear is creeping back inside
Here I go again flooded with fear
Pain and shame fill each tear
The storm is coming dark and fierce
Standing and gazing my eyes pierce
I am sure this is just another level of healing
And maybe for a lifetime I will be dealing
This pain only subsides with a touch
And it's yours I long for so much
It's you my heart is open too
Holding me is just not something you do
So my heart wanders
And my mind wonders
I lift this pen and take to paper
Praying this dissipates like vapor
Many men would hold and caress
leave me settling for less
My body longs to be held by strength
Arms of safety at any length
A chest to lean
And stability to glean
My soul yearns for this the most
Actually not me... The Holy Ghost
My body longs for earthly emptiness
But His Spirit resides in me yearning for the Eternal
Greatness
When I focus on what I can touch, hear, taste, and see
I come up short, hurt, and empty
Even now reminded connection to You is Key
Awaiting my transcendence
Forever consumed in Your presence

Too Much

How do I free myself of this chaos?
Worries fears a sense of loss
Questioning every part of me
I wish I could understand and then maybe
Maybe I could stop the hyper vigilance
Ongoing assessing to change up my stance
Constant interpretation of attitudes, words, and
interaction
I can't seem to stop the evaluation
Fear, control, and defenses
Only leads to false pretenses
Looking for the hidden purpose and motive
Looking for validity before I can give
It's not only interaction with others
Thoughts of my deficits smothers
Whether it is about my shape and size
This stomach my arms and thighs
Or mistakes made as a parent
Dysfunction or pain I never meant
Roles of leadership and responsibility given
I know they see my spark I'm driven
Driven by insecurities and fears of being good enough
I wish I could let go of all this stuff
My head is full about to explode
I need a break from myself, put me in relaxation mode

Races

My mind races
Sometimes in circles and different paces
Wondering about providing, parenting and relationship
skills
Life seems to be an ongoing journey of various hills
At times swallowed by inadequacy
I wonder what will I leave what will be my legacy
Sometimes I'm too much for myself to bare
How could I expect someone else to stay and be there?
It's like getting stuck in a deep dark hole
Alone isolated with a marred soul
Just give me a scarlet letter
Or I will yell unclean unclean like the lepers that would be
better
Wanting so bad to belong
But this pull to safe isolation is strong
I don't want you to see all my flaws
I feel them regularly the shame gnaws
The emotions feelings are a blessing and curse
And I know it could be worse
I just want out of my skin
I don't know where this is coming from when did it begin
My smile tends to light up a room
Now it's darkness and gloom
I want to curl up in fetal position
To numb out and not feel this affliction
If I could lay my head on your chest
To feel your heart beat and your arms rest
On the small of my back as you rub away the fears
I would let out some of this pain and tears
I'm not sure that hours would be enough
God I am so tired of being strong and tough
Can I fall apart and just be weak
Can I get this anger out and the truth speak
I'm tired and need you to heal me within

No more comfort in Maryjane or gin
No more running or cutting folks out
I need you to teach me help me and show me what this is
all about

Darkness

The heaviness is returning
Pain inside still burning
Tears well like water against the banks
Trying to regain hope and give thanks
A shadow of darkness is calling
Taunting, drawing me I'm falling
Feel the need to retreat
Will I ever shake this or will it always beat
On my Spirit on my being
From its grasp I can't find freeing
Maybe this is my thorn
It just comes no forewarn
Makes me sick to go so low
Feels weak what if they know
How the darkness consumes
My past it exhumes
I am unaware of its purpose
I just know it makes the pain resurface
Is it a purging of my innermost?
Or just a trap to have engrossed

Depression

Out of this depression I have to come
Tired of feeling so numb
Overtaken by the pain of the past
Dear God how long will this last
I know that healing isn't painless
Praying all this has purpose and isn't meaningless
My mind is in a dark place
No joy or peace not a trace
The past is over now
I need to let it go somehow
Its memories Engraved in me
Its scars you can plainly see
The present has enough pains of its own
Adding to the weight I already bare
Somehow this doesn't seem fair
I want to let go but how
I want to be whole right now!
No longer affected by wounds of another
Freeing me to be a good friend and mother

Numb

Retreating is so familiar
Hiding helps my head get clearer
The solitude sucks me in
Sometimes wanting to shed my own skin
escape these thoughts in my head
Curl up trapped in my bed
Pain wells up and consumes my being
a little numbing would be so freeing
Just for a moment or as long as it last
old skeletons from my past
taunting me with their quick fix solutions
Just an escape I need resolution

Let Go

Let go of the past
Or its painful grip will last
Look back only for the truth you can find
For a short while or to it you will bind
Forgive understand and make amends where you can
Then move on no need to look at it again
Let it go and live in the present
Free yourself from any resentment
Love like it's your first
For Peace and good hunger and thirst
Talk to the Creator throughout your day
Listen and watch for what He will say
Lay your fears and hurts at his feet
And in His presence regularly retreat
Trust that He knows and has something better
This is my letter
To remind me to let go of the past
So its painful grip won't last
To look around at what I have today
It's much greater than my yesterday!

Control

I told her about my ongoing sleepless nights
And how I am trying to get this shit right
Let go meditate calm down relax they say
I wish I could I wish my brain would work this way
She told me it sounds like anxiety
Hypervigilance, brain like a spinning top describe to a tee
She said your writing that's good
Now write about control if you could
No medications to sedate
I don't care I just want this gone a clean slate
I am sure as a baby in my play pen
Curdled bottle of milk I know this is way back when
I wonder if she heard my cry
To be held fed or for my diaper to be dry
I wonder if I longed to be wrapped in their arms
Whispered promises of protections from all harms
I wonder if I felt powerless
When they took me from my home pitiless
Control of my physical being
Seems like daily her dominance I was dealing
With no one to turn to
Protect me from the wounds won't you!
Questions I had answers looking for
Met with harsh words and a closed door
Powerless over where my life started
Understanding my parents and why they departed
Looking for connection approval affirmation
Mouth shut, acts to please never enough for her
perfection
There was no place I could be sure
Sure about me my life no ...just tainted impure
Floating no connection
Aboding fear of her chastisement and rejection
I felt like I had no control over me

The way I thought felt and wanted to be
My being dictated by a greater source
Her fears perception insecurities she would enforce
Powerless over the labels of things I was not
Liar, not good enough, fat, whore nothing this was my lot
I froze completely
The night he took my virginity
Even in this I was to blame
The cause of family shame
I felt in control of nothing
I had to turn to something
No human was there to protect
I had not heard from God so Him I would reject
I soon found that weed could be my cure
And it did it helped me endure
I soon gained control through my rebellion
For these acts I should receive a medallion
I gained control of my defenses
I refined them over and over enhancing my senses
Never did I see how my control was failing
Binding my heart and mind ailing
Beginning to see glimpses of its destruction
Beginning to see its dysfunction

Battered heart

The battered heart a delicate thing
Words that were said cut and sting
The intentional silence
This is your penance
a child in a boxing match
Standbyer's offer a band aid an watch
Innocence and vulnerability we didn't know
Heart wide open blow after blow
Deprived of acceptance
We were unworthy this our sentence
Abuse we endured we asked for
No protection just more
Some were completely knocked out
Some kept getting in the ring with a shout
Hearts wouldn't stop dreaming
Fighting heart wide open beaming
I will win someone will love this damaged heart
Blind with hope struck with another dart
Wounds are infected now
I can't smell the putrid smell somehow
Blind to how the infection has set in
just pain crippling from within
Desperately ignorantly I find some relief
A twist in this concoction
Soothing never healing the infliction
With every soothing action
Further I get from an honest reflection
When these potions and elixirs lose their power
Like they always do like a dying flower
I begin to feel see the cost
Begin to see all I have lost
With each sip inhale unemotional fuck
I am still in the ring getting struck
Every act of denial and temporary filling
I'm still getting beat and blood I'm still spilling...

Mold

The mold is being broken
With every word he has spoken
His being shows clear the cracks
Of the strength the mold lacks
A protective outer shell
Keeping me in my own hell
I fight the urge to run
His smile like the morning sun
Drawing me to his heart
Oh God break this mold apart
Show me my true being
No longer through this darkness will I be seeing
Who I am and my true reflection
Now is clear give me time for inspection
So tender is my being to touch
Shedding the mold I realize I have missed so much
Sensitive to all that surrounds me
So alive I see so clearly
A new birth a new chance
Free to love and free to dance
No mold holding me in or holding me back

Winning

I'm so tired it's the end of my day
Not enough energy to play
Always enough to write down these ideas though
They seem to come with little effort they just flow
I wonder when the writing will change
So many things to write I think it is strange
My kids, my God, recovery
Life experiences and self-discovery
Right now just love fears and childhood
I would like to say I'm all good
But that would be deception
Going through a process trying to change my perception
On what my life has been
Not sure I want to do it again
So my story I am reflecting
My experiences I am respecting
Each one for a reason and purposes
Maybe just for now so I can right these verses
Revealing hurts and trauma
Trying to release what's inside no more drama
Letting go from the past the binds
Maybe helping others clear their minds
No longer holding this pain within
I'm getting stronger from the past I will win

Pressing

Feels like a weight pressing on my heart
Speaking my truth trying to do my part
Asking for help I never use to do
Trusting people only a few
Ongoing fear people will go away
The pain is overwhelming I'm filled with dismay
I feel it in my chest
Not feeling my best
Throat getting tight
No end in sight
I begin to feel hopeless in what it is I have to face
Can I put things in perspective in their proper place?
My responses to some I don't understand
Please just take my hand
Trying to get better
So I keep writing these letters
Will my life remain this way?
I just want to be okay
To be able to trust and not retreat
This childhood loss I have to beat

Bound

I'm bound by limits no matter my state
No matter how much I desire to be free this is my fate
Bound by my unheard voice
Bound by my past and choice
Bound by fears and failures
Bound by this pain that endures
Bound by shame and guilt
Bound by the lack of foundation built
Bound by my human condition
Bound by my inconsistent motivation
Bound by responsibilities
Bound by my insecurities
Bound by money
Bound by the dream of callin you honey
Bound by societies laws and expectations
Bound by people's interpretations
Bound by genetics
Bound by these tendencies characteristics
Bound by abilities
Bound by human frailties
Bound by gender
Bound by being fat or slender
Bound by ethnicity and race
Bound by time and space
Bound by an order and system
Bound by materialism

Bound by deadlines
Bound by the news and daily headline
Bound by the weather
Bound by things I just can't get together
I'm bound I'm bound
In more ways than these I have found
I am human I have limitations that are binding
Even in this writing bound by the words I am finding
I am bound by limits no matter my state

I am human ...this is my fate

Release

A night of release
Words a flirtatious tease
If I close my eyes and listen to your voice
Getting lost in your painted words would be my choice
It's not just the words alone
It the dreams and ideas that are sown
Your body in response to what flows
The rhythm in your speech everyone knows
A   piece of you has been purged
Now meaning and purpose have emerged
I want to live more
My life is where my words are store

Solitude

It's the solitude of my room I greet
Words start to stream across the paper I retreat
Somewhere I have never been
My mind stops racing and then
Peace and contentment begin to fill
I can be quiet and just sit still
Nothing else in the world seems to matter
I don't even hear all the other chitter chatter
Its then my soul seems free to speak
Vulnerably and openly never leaving me weak
In fact a healing and strength from whatever comes out
Never knowing what the writing is going to be about
I realize just now I am no longer afraid to feel
Because through this writing I have begun to heal
To depths no therapist, preacher, or book could provide
My healing and gift are one they coincide
I am so thankful for the finding
Nothing on my own I keep reminding
I have looked for solutions and freedom everywhere
All along inside of me I was so foolish unaware
Everything I need is right here within
Ready to live this life fully ready to begin

Recovery

Sometimes I hate recovery
it's the powerlessness and discovery
The things out of my control
The damage and how it has taken a toll
In every part of my being
The destruction and dysfunction I'm seeing
I didn't ask to be born
And what I have is like another thorn
Another imperfection
Spreads like infection
I'm sick and I hate it
I didn't create it!!
I'm pissed because I've been prayin
I'm pissed because I've admitted and been sayin
God I can't fix this
I try but I'm amiss
I'm trying to find my way ... I'm lost
Seeking truth and healing a painful cost
Relationship starts and ends
My shit limits my friends
Draws them close and pushes away
Torment of needing and isolation raised this way
I want badly to break free from my past
Relief comes and goes I want it to last
Moments of sanity and clarity
Just can't tolerate the times of disparity
It's the powerlessness and discovery
Sometimes I hate recovery

Pain

Pain is a guaranteed experience
In fact a regular occurrence
Your religion or race it does not discriminate
Gender, single, or have a mate
Mansion on the hill or in the projects
Pain has no preference no specific subjects
Education or none makes no difference
Your paths will cross just have patience
Raised by one two or more
Parentless it has no mercy it will be at your door
Pain goes past the visible
So deep indescribable
Infects your mind
So great...escape is what you try to find
Scars your heart
Tears you apart
A pain in your stomach and knot in your throat
Makes you want to run go somewhere remote
Causes you to question the Creator
Let me know You are there an indicator!
Pain causes you to lash out at your lover
Your words hurt they run for cover
Pain will have you searching for a cure
A numbing potion sure!

Pain will have you spend all you got
In attempts to fill that spot
Pain will have you seek a crutch
In a man or woman's touch
Pain can make you shut the world out
People asking what's wrong what this is all about
Pain will make you think no one understands
Make you shout and throw up your hands
Pain brings a sense of powerlessness
Cause you to feel a little less
Like you should be able to handle this on your own
So use to saying I got this I'm grown
Pain can lead to death and destruction
Make you feel crazy like you can't function
It will leave its mark a forever stain
A guaranteed part of life.....pain

Family

Baby Girl

My heart hurts a little when I think of what we missed
No hugs no forehead kissed
No you're a princess daddy's little girl
No dances or ballerina twirl
My heart aches deep
And my eyes I can't keep
The tears from filling
No daddy's wisdom instilling
My heart hurts for you
And that little girl in me too
The reality of not having a daddy to do what daddy's do
Strong arms of protection to help you through
Protector and provider
Always there as a life guider
Some of these as your mom I can do and will
But a father's role I can never fulfill
I can only pray that God fills that part of your heart
You're so beautiful funny and smart
All too well do I know?
How having a daddy would help you grow
Abba please feel this need
With You alone do I plead

My First

I wondered when this writing would come
Finally it is here I will share it with some
But for you my child that's who this is for
These words bursting up coming from my core
The bond began as soon as I knew about your creation
I know for some things I did there was no explanation
I was a child carrying a child
And me well still quite wild
Down the school halls waddling while I walk
Whispering voices with their words of judgment talk
I didn't care
I had you there
Even in my womb you gave me strength
I knew I had to fight to go any length
To protect and provide
My love for you I would not hide
You grew feet kicking my rib
I was so proud of your Winnie the pooh crib
Let me get to the point of this rhyme
I'm reminiscing now taking some time
I had you when I was 17yrs old
Your worth to me more than gold
I know I wasn't great at always showing it
Running from here to there I couldn't quit
I wish I had taken more time to just be with you
So fast so quick you grew
Before I knew it my gift was gone
Never that duckling always a swan
You grew and off to college you went
So amazed by you ...wish I had spent

More time enjoying you and your laughter
Your wit and determination qualities I was after
Your talents bring me to tears
And your wisdom beyond your years
You possess a strength like no other
It exciting to watch you discover
New things and places
New passions and faces
Truths about the world and life
I really wish I could have and could keep you from all strife
Where you could be untouched from the world dangers
and harm
If there were a potion necklace or charm!
That could guarantee
Your body mind and heart safety
Oh baby girl I would but it!
But you probably wouldn't try it or wear it shit
Who am I kidding' your my child
Experiencing life and a bit wild
I love you
To your heart stay true
Keep living life to its fullest
When I see you I will pull you to my chest
And hold you so tightly
And continue to pray morning and nightly!

Prodigal Son

I wonder if this is how You feel
Watching us make bad choices and deals
Bargaining our future for this moments desire
So head strong and unwilling anguish is what we require
Physical pain emotional torment and spiritual emptiness
You give us a choice but we keep creating mess
No amount of love could cause us to see
No not until we get to that place on blended knee
The dangers and death like Russian roulette
No telling the countless times you intervened I bet
It must pain You to see us do what we do
Unnecessary pain and separation from You
God I beg You to watch over your son
You know him and all he has done
I know You have a plan and purpose for him
But his choices and situations makes things look dim
I'm trusting You
Keep him in the palm of Your hand like the Word promises
You do
He is Your child
Untamed and wild
But he has a calling and a purpose
We can all see it there is no fooling us
Please remove the enemies grip on him
This pain is great I'm filled to the brim
I have no answers but to call on You
Please come in change deliver and rescue
Prepare his mind and heart
To be willing and ready for a new start
You are all knowing Sovereign and wise
Trusting You with our son a priceless prize

Blue Eyes

My Blue eyed baby boy
In my life you bring much joy
In my arms I do hold
Since you were little but now too old
Growing up so big and fast
My love for you will forever last
Your heart so big and so forgiving
I pray you stay that way all you're living
Being outside with your friends
Kissing me goodnight is how the day ends
Oh these days won't last
Soon will be a thing of the past
Mom can we go fishing
Mom can I have this.... I have been wishing
Mom I need some cash
Mom come here I got this rash
Broken bones and er trips
Life lessons and romance tips
I would teach you
And you would teach me out of the blue
A boy through and through
Doing what good boys do
Eating not stop
Playing football til you drop
Boy go take a shower
Mom can I have another hour
So busy wanting to go here and there
Always helpful showing you care
Praying I can give you a good start
I love you Taylor with all my heart

Father's Day

Today is a day of special recognition
A day of yearly tradition
A time to honor our father or fathers
Presents wrapped, food cooked, family gathers
One day of the year we express to dad
How great he is and impression he has had
For many this will be the first
And for some their worst
You see not everyone grows
Watching dad tie his ties or bows
Cutting the grass and reading the Sunday paper
Going to the barbershop gettin that fade that taper
Yet others do
Their bond was tight and it grew!
Then one day unexpected
He was gone and everyone was affected
The pain of his loss to great
So much you questioned your own fate
Now here you are year or years later
Still with a hole the size of a crater
I'm not sure what is more terrible
Both pains so deep inexpressible
An uninvolved father living
Or a good father now grieving

....so father's you need to know we love you
Whether present, absent, or in the heavens in the blue
We need you everyday
We miss being able to call and say what we say
Dads that are distant
Don't take your role for granted not for an instant
Being a dad is no small call
You're needed by us all
Dad's that are doing it the best you know how
Take today be encouraged regain your strength now
And for you men that are filling in the gap
We honor you and give you an applause a hand clap
Happy father's day to those who have passed, are absent,
or present

Fathers

Your presence was ordained from above
Cover your family with protection and love
Be that voice of wisdom and rational
Walking example strength and inspirational
Demonstrating the way boys become a man
Teaching the girls how to be treated and Gods plan
Respect, perseverance, commitment, integrity
Confidence, perspective, and spiritual humility
How to lead and serve
When to act and when to observe!
When did you determine you weren't needed
When to those doubts and fears you heeded
That you might not be strong enough
That at times it was just tough to be tough
That you didn't always have a solution
And doubted the impact of your contribution
That things out of your control would happen
And the burden is heavy even for the captain
That at times you would make mistakes
And you would have to share in the heart aches
Is this when you decided?
Is this when your calling collided?
With your fears and insecurity
Causing you to engage in permanent infidelity?

Let me be a voice of reason
A father is not just for a season
It is a commitment forever
Not even Death can take this a way ...nothing never!
Your absence leaves scars
Leaving your children behind metal and mental bars
Looking for things to replace
That hole you left the gapping space
search filled with emptiness and destruction
You were designed to be a part of my construction!
Sons guessing at what it is to be a man
Resorted to making babies with no means no plan
Running the streets chasing money
Earning respect returning in body bags bloody
Filled with confusion coming out as hate
No queens just increased domestic violence rate
Daughters need you too a few things to mention
Looking too men to give her daddy's attention
Not seeing her own beauty
Lowered herself from queen to booty
Used by men over and over
knows no better cuz you never told her
Early on she realizes she has to do this on her own
16 17 actin like she's grown
Her independence some see as good
Really it's her lack of trust misunderstood
When to those doubts and fears you heeded
When did you determine you weren't needed

Life

There have been times of bad choices
Times of nothing but rejoices
My Creator has always been near
I have strayed in independence and fear
Two more children would soon come along
For the road ahead I would need to be strong
A husband who struggles with his own demons
I did all I could, I had to leave I had reasons
Four children now we ventured to Tennessee
The accent was strong and everyone called me sweetie
The children adapted okay
Uprooted from their home but in Tennessee we would
stay
New school new friends new home
I tried to make it fun so we would roam
Downtown, Lake Radnor, and Centennial Park
New life new adventures we would embark
Memories of what we left I try to forget
Attempts to move forward with no regret
Still the past haunts me now
Ripple effect of my choices wish I could fix somehow
My Creator continues to protect and provide
I know He is with me at my side

Helping me with my family
Giving us a life where we can live happily
Life has been a bit of a roller coaster
Where I am today I cannot boaster
Despite my losses and history
He didn't have to do it open all these doors for me
I have made a lot of bad calls
Gotten some bruises had a lot of falls
But my God is always right there
Sometimes with a hand and sometimes with an
encouraging stare
His faith in me is great
I don't know what it is but He sees my fate
I am thankful for my life's story
Any good He gets that glory!

Oil & Vinegar

Unclaimed

I cannot rid myself of this gloom that comes to steal my
gratitude
This aching in my soul I can't deny
This wanton heart unfulfilled
I try to shush her and tell her to calm down
I scold her for being ungrateful for what she has been
given
I shake her in disgust why can't you just be happy
As shame and guilt overtake tears slowly begin to drip
then flow
My heart is discontent as I sit in the church pew alone
My heart feels isolated in a crowd of couples at each
child's performance or game
My heart feels rejected and unclaimed
No love to miss me when I am gone
No love excited to see me come through the door
No companion to plan the next adventure
No lover to dream about the future
My heart longs to be claimed
An orphaned heart
Good, loyal, giving, and caring and sometimes selfless
Longs to be joined to one that will love her, protect her
Live and experience life with
Joys and sorrows
Arguments and laughs
Late night conversations and early morning trips
I try to shush her this unclaimed heart of mine

Deep in my chest

My heart has dropped deep in my chest
My throat is tight and I am trying my best
To not let these tears fall
To keep my head up and stand tall
Because I know the best love
Is like the one from up above
Freely given freely received
But my heart I am sorry has given birth conceived
Thoughts of you leaving when I want you to stay
I feel like retreating running away
If I could keep my heart locked
Build a wall keep these emotions blocked
To go through life a little more numb
Maybe the fantasy of love I would no longer succumb
Able to live a life with no care
No more glowing from your stare
No more waiting in anticipation
For hints or signs for this thing taking manifestation

Daydreams

I wonder in the time of his day do I appear in his
daydreams
In his quiet does he hear my laugh
When he walks on the beach does he wish me at his side
Alone on the couch does he miss my touch
When his hand grazes his lips does he feel mine
When he is gone does he wish I was there
Do random thoughts of me brighten his eyes
Does he reminisce about our building history
Does he imagine us
Is life better with me in his
In his solitude does he fear losing it
When I leave does he prefer I stay...
I just wonder

Different

This is so different than the rest
I mean really it's been the best
This is no circus no amusement park
I mean this one is gonna leave a positive mark
Slow and steady
Neither of which was I ready
Overwhelmed with what I am just now see in'
Actually free in'
Ms. Mills sang she never knew a love like this before
The past is gone a closed door
Your the tortoise I'm the hare
But your love none can compare
Your endurance and loyalty are a rare gift
Your quick wit and smile my spirits lift
Your love is without question
Your brazen truth only for my edification
All this time but I feel the guard coming down
Sorry it's taken me so long to come around
Sorry for fightin' the love you were givin'
See me lovin' you sure but you lovin' me I was disbelievin'
There had to be a catch
Tainted love I've had my fill they seem to attach
females come trying to catch your time your eye
Can't blame them so do I
But it's me you give it too
Damn I love you
I just couldn't ask for anything better
Trying to find a way to tell you so I wrote this letter
Thank you for loving me
For staying when you could have just let me be
You have showed me a love I never knew
And I won't be the same because of you

Intoxicated

Drowning in love
Consumed by its intoxication
Basking in its glow
Pumping through my veins
Makes my toes wiggle and feet dance
Makes my thick thighs and curves sexy
Twist in my hips as I walk
Shoulders back
Chest confidently out
Head held high love
Arms sway freely
Heart pumps intensely
Air fills my lungs
My breathe is deep in and out
Mind clear
Gaze is sure and piercing
Words come forth strong and true
Spirit alive
Leaping within
Senses heightened
Love is consuming me now

You

Our initial meeting random
Year later I meet you so handsome
But business it was
So I kept a distance because
I didn't want to seem like a desperate chick
One you could love and leave real quick
But your lips and smile had me in a daze
And that chocolate skin I could forever gaze
You smile and intellect had my attention
There wasn't anything to you I could not mention
Conversations that last for hours
Chemistry unstoppable powers
Not referring to sexual healing
But being able to open up and share your feeling
Thoughts ideas and passions flow between us
The world family beliefs we would discuss
Eyes opening to another point of view
You seeing things about me I never knew
Making me aware of areas I could grow
My strengths and abilities you seem to also know
I have never known this kind of openness
Still trying to grasp that you won't love me less
Dreaming about you throughout the day
Waiting for your call to hear what you have to say
I wonder at times what the future holds
I experience you amazed as this unfolds
I cannot lie I do have some fears
It seems I have searched for this for years
Now that I have what I have wanted in the past
Will I be able to handle it so it can last?
So inexperienced in this thing called love
But what you have I know I want a lot of

Intrigued

You came you were intrigued by me and I didn't know why
Just another story passing you by
You asked me questions and remembered every detail
I said I used to be ...and you replied you will without fail
Your interest in me was genuine and pure
Not like anything I ever endured
Conversation went on for hours into the night
First me and then you thoughts and ideas shedding light
You made sure to treat me with care
Holding the door, paying the tab....so rare
Words of comfort and assurance that you would be there
That I no longer had to do this life being so unaware
Of my beauty worth and strength
My need for trust and truth
You said there was nothing I could do to gain what I
wanted from you
You waited and pleaded just be through
With the wall you have hid behind for so long
Take off the masks you don't have to be strong
Give me what's real and true....
Acceptance is what I have been given from a few
I know this is just the beginning
I pray with no quick ending
Never knew this is how it could be
What a priceless gift you have given me

Thoughts of you

Thoughts of you enter my mind
I wonder if true love is what we will find
I can't help it, wondering is what I do
Can't help but wonder if true love will be found with you
Hopeless romantic I may be
Can't help it something inside of me
Yearns for that deep connection
I'm not asking for the world's perfection
Just something true and real
Something both of us can feel
I don't want to force it I know it will take some time
Wanting that deeper connection I don't think is a crime
Someone who will understand
Someone who will help me expand
No not in size
I mean my life help me realize
Those things maybe I just don't see
Like when love comes close I tend to flee
Or those attributes I tend to doubt
He would patiently encourage and watch them come
about
Someone to add strength to who I already am
Has my back won't leave me in a jam
This isn't one way, two-way street is a must
Mutual support mutual trust
Day dreaming is what I do
Wondering if you do too

Wait

Faced with the question is he the right one
And if not should I just be done
So much he has taught me
To be open with myself to be free
I wonder if closeness will come in time
Or will I continue writing rhyme after rhyme
About my feelings wants and desire
He fuels it like fire
I need his body close to feel his touch
But maybe for him this is too much
His words of affirmation and support
My longing and needs I don't want to distort
Two are stronger than one I believe
I know this may be difficult for you to receive
Maybe I'm looking to lean on you
A bit more than you're ready to do
I wonder if I wait
Will all this come or dissipate

Heart of a man

Who really knows the heart of a man?
Fears, dreams, longings, doubts ...no one can
Who can understand the thoughts of his mind?
Searching this earth hoping to find
Endless and futile this hunt
Waste of time sorry to be so blunt
No one knows why I do what I do
And at the end of the day who cares? Do you?
Our stories some similarities
Every being so complex ... many disparities
I can't expect you to understand me or this writing
Leads to quarrels and fighting
Individuality now defined
The best I can do is open my mind
Each one uniquely designed
Looking to my Father for what I need
Trying to trust and follow His lead

Express

How do I express the way I feel about you?
If words could that's what I would do
But they get twisted and fall short
I need something else to support
If I could pierce our hearts just a little
We could both see inside it would be no riddle
Plain as day ....as the sky is blue
No more questions, doubt, or subtle clue
If presents or presence would explain
How deep this is ...I can't refrain
I'm lost because what I can do isn't the answer either
Cooking cleaning neither
Shaking my head in dismay
There has to be a way
For you to know without a doubt
That I love you and what I am about
If I could hide myself in your arms and chest
Seeking safety protection and rest
I would stay there as long as I could
Probably much longer than I should
I don't want to exhaust you
I just want to know that you really knew
That I understand the significance of your uniqueness
And sometimes you need a break from humans just to
decompress
Your firm in your ways and beliefs
You questions religiosity to many thief's
That breaking the mold and being against the grain
Is how you are and I hope you remain
A non-conformist at its finest
And just a bit of a perfectionist
Time is money and both are precious
Verbal and nonverbal outspokenness

Holding a mirror so I can see my attributes and flaws
Standing next to me your acceptance draws
Right is right and wrong is wrong
Respect for talent funk will always be your song
Loyalty and sensitivity to those around you
Not from this world just making a debut
This is the man on earth that knows me best
Provokes me and challenges me to rise to the test
This is the man
The one I want in my future plan

Reckless

My heart knows it's desire
But it is untamed reckless like fire
Seeking and searching for a love of its own
Loves like a child forgetting I'm grown
Settling for the love you give
Leaves me longing please forgive
Loving big is what I do
I need this back and want it from you
Can't make you love another way
Time will tell if we stay
So for now I will step back
See if you can fill those areas of lack
Restraining is hard for me
Because in your arms is where I want to be
Seeking love from those that can't quite give it
Reoccurring story that I permit
Consciously or not this is my reality
Unfulfilling painful normality
So I wonder what would happen
If I could tame this desire passion
Reel it in until the stars aligned
Hold on to my love for the one designed

A Little Broken

My heart is a little broken
From the words that have been spoken
Call me what you want
And with evasive ideas taunt
Telling me you're direct
But then explain things with some other type of intellect
Insightful words and ideas you spit at me
I just want to hear you say with me is where you want to
be
Don't leave my mind to wonder
Make my heart pound like thunder
You say it's me who isn't ready
But I think it's your mind that is not steady
You say you don't have time to be wasting
But you run from love you could be embracing
My heart hurts even to write these words
But shit you said we were grown this is for the birds!!
Wanting me to be myself
Then making me feel like I should sit quietly on the shelf
Waiting for what I'm not knowing
One day I think we are growing
And the next I'm just company
Might as well pull out your black book you got me!
There is no doubt how I feel about you!
If there was anything I could do I do
I'm open telling you how I feel
With no response like it's not a big deal
Sure my love has its flaws
By my God you have seen them all
So tell me what's going on in your heart
Let me know what direction to start

He sees

He sees things in me
Thoughts and ways that keep me from being free
I wonder will he love me with all these deficits
Or will I always feel like I belong with the rejected misfits
Wandering about this life
Looking for acceptance only to find pain and strife
He engages in my self-exploration
I become consumed with deep adoration
But now a sudden twist?
My heart begins to race and my eyes mist
Then a calmness reassured
While my history speaks to what I have endured
A love for him has begun
I am comforted knowing true love won't run
So time will tell what this will be
For now I will keep discovering me
If he stays or if he goes
There are a few things I know
To open my heart to loves possibilities
While healing from past travesties
To be true to who I am
And everything doesn't end in a sham!
I have learned that life is give and take
And I must open myself up if good friends are what I want
to make
You have opened my eyes to things that are new
That will forever change what I do
For today I won't worry if you could love me too
I am sure time will show me what to do

Heart on Lock

So disconnected from your own
Mine are too much when they are shown
I have been open in how I feel
In fact I have told you a great deal
Letting you in to see my fears
Showing you my heart and my tears
This is a gift not many get
Something you can't do yet
So because of yours you deny
Your too emotional will always be your reply
You're so passionate and so deep
I wish your heart you would not keep
Hidden away so the world won't touch
Not even knowing it's a crutch
The love you were taught
So many have sought
And you have it guarded safely under lock
Unaware how this causes you alone to walk

I Thought

I say I'm in love
He says girl you don't know until u receive it from above
Leaving me in wonder speechless
This man knows my heart and loves me no less
My shortcomings and strengths
He says love knows no bounds no lengths
Loyalty when running seems the only option
Honesty the kind that is raw gives true reflection
No labels to define
Just choice to commit is his and mine
Individuality staying true to one's self
Yet showing concern about my commonwealth
Encouragement to explore my talents and gifts
In his presence or absence my heart lifts
Its value more than the world's riches
If this isn't love I don't know what is

Love to Move

I want love to move free
Through to and out of me
I want life to be vibrant and full
Playful and meaningful
To love and live with no limit
No time no fear to prohibit
Feeling each moment taking it in
Close my eyes letting myself imagine
The power of eagle wings in my arms
Soaring high away from all harms
Or next to the stream let's go
With the water ebb and flow
A sense of peace consumes me now
Heart beating at a steady pace I vow
To never turn back
No more searching for what I lack
Because I have it right here within
Since the beginning of time and my creation
A plan and a purpose
No longer feeling worthless
With confidence and strength I stand
Now willing to take your hand
Because I have these gifts in me
Meant to bless us both you see
So I will let go and let life take its course
No need to control or force
Feeling the wind on my face
No concern for time or place
Watching the water with closed eyes
Calming sounds no surprise
One with my Creator today
In His blessed presence I'll stay

I wonder

I wonder if he even knows
How my draw to him grows
I wonder if he is aware
Of his influence on my hearts repair
Does he know how daydreams of him fill my mind?
Does he know this is rare not common to find
He inspires me to be me
Showing me the chords that keep me from being free
Encourages me with the truth
Helped me face pains of my youth
He doesn't know his influence
I know our meeting wasn't coincidence
He adds happiness to my life
My expressions cause him strife
The words of endearment
For him words of discouragement
I'm at a loss, this is overflowing from the inside
The feelings I want to express and can't hide
I want to share the impact you make
Maybe you think my words are fake
I open my heart and the words are true
But when they hit your ears somehow a misconstrue
I am looking at the progress of our relationship
While you thank the Creator you're not in a partnership
I wonder where the lines were crossed
This is not the reaction I expected your emotions I exhaust
I am taken back to square one
I am too much and maybe with me you are done....

Beautiful

I want to be beautiful to him
Whether the lights are bright or dim
Feel his hands run across my skin
I don't care where he starts as long as he begins
I'm a whole lot of woman see
Wanting to be desired mind spirit and body
Yearning to feel his hand hold my cheek
His approval is deeply what I seek
Take my body and complete your inspections
Show me your desire despite the imperfections
Take your fingers hands lips and tongue
no reservations cause I'm already sprung
Your satisfaction is my desire
I want you to burn for me burn like fire

Deep in my chest

My heart has dropped deep in my chest
My throat is tight and I am trying my best
To not let these tears fall
To keep my head up and stand tall
Because I know the best love
Is like the one from up above
Freely given freely received
But my heart I am sorry has given birth conceived
Thoughts of you leaving when I want you to stay
I feel like retreating running away
If I could keep my heart locked
Build a wall keep these emotions blocked
To go through life a little more numb
Maybe the fantasy of love I would no longer succumb
Able to live a life with no care
No more glowing from your stare
No more waiting in anticipation
For hints or signs for this thing taking manifestation

Wonder

I wonder if he is my husband or another lesson
This unknown future at times has me stressin'
I wonder if he is my Prince Charming
Or will he soon my heart be harming...
I wonder is he my forever
Or my almost not quite meaningful endeavor
I wonder if our future will no longer be a mystery
Or will it end up being a part of my history
I wonder to much I suppose
It's not that I am trying to impose
But you see my heart is there
I wish I could plan you know prepare
For what might not be
For future heartache I can't see
Reality is whether he stay or go
And whatever I do or don't know
Whether it's now, later, or never
I just don't want that hurt not again not ever

Speak

What if his silence could speak
What words would he use what emotions would leak
His heart is hidden deep in his chest
Locked away from the rest
A safe distance from the world he keeps
His claim the black sheep of sheeps
Maybe so ... There is truth to his uniqueness
Never show any signs of pain, vulnerability, or weakness
Maybe this is what your silence explains
His separation and isolation contains
Love, loss, hopes, brokenness, his heart
A wall has been built to keep it safe and set apart
Sometimes it weakens and his heart shines through
But each time he has quickly withdrew
I think he has before given his heart away
And now keeps it locked up so safe it will stay
Maybe at one time he showed vulnerability
And fear, pain, or rejection caused an insecurity
Maybe true love pierced his heart
Vowing never again to feel so torn apart
Maybe it was the loss of someone close and dear
Never again would he get so close let one so near
Or maybe it is just the world we live in
So filled with corruption

Corruption of the mind body and soul
Maybe all of it has just taken its toll
He is so strong and sure
Certainly he has been equipped to endure
I wish I could be the one to help tear down the wall
Could I be gentle and patient enough? I would have to start small
Who am I kidding that is no place for me
Only a work for the Creator and he
Lord I pray you wrestle with my love
I pray for divine intervention and healing from above
Speak to his inner man in his silence
Open his ears to hear through all the worlds turbulence
Give him wisdom, courage, and willingness
Good health and continue to bless
Let him find favor wherever he goes
And protect him from his head to his toes
Take his distance and his heart
Hold him close and never depart

You

Thoughts of you enter my mind
I wonder if true love is what we will find
I can't help it, wondering is what I do
Can't help but wonder if true love will be found with you
Hopeless romantic I may be
Can't help it something inside of me
Yearns for that deep connection
I'm not asking for the world's perfection
Just something true and real
Something both of us can feel
I don't want to force it I know it will take some time
Wanting that deeper connection I don't think is a crime
Someone who will understand
Someone who will help me expand
No not in size
I mean my life help me realize
Those things maybe I just don't see
Like when love comes close I tend to flee
Or those attributes I tend to doubt
He would patiently encourage and watch them come
about
Someone to add strength to who I already am
Has my back won't leave me in a jam
This isn't one way, two-way street is a must
Mutual support mutual trust
Day dreaming is what I do
Wondering if you do too

Does He Know?

I wonder if he knows
I wonder if he even knows
How my draw to him grows
I wonder if he is aware
Of his influence on my hearts repair
Does he know how daydreams of him fill my mind?
Does he know this is rare not common to find
He inspires me to be me
Showing me the chords that keep me from being free
Encourages me with the truth
Helped me face pains of my youth
He doesn't know his influence
I know our meeting wasn't coincidence
He adds happiness to my life
My expressions cause him strife
The words of endearment
For him words of discouragement
I'm at a loss, this is overflowing from the inside
The feelings I want to express and can't hide
I want to share the impact you make
Maybe you think my words are fake
I open my heart and the words are true
But when they hit your ears somehow a misconstrue
I am looking at the progress of our relationship
While you thank the Creator you're not in a partnership
I wonder where the lines were crossed
This is not the reaction I expected your emotions I exhaust
I am taken back to square one
I am too much and maybe with me you are done….

Linger

Strange how thoughts of you seem to linger in my mind
No cue no words needed to remind
Taken residence right in my heart
I can feel you even when we are apart
Sometimes even more intensely then when we are
together
Feeling filled with you no matter the weather
I wish these words could fully express
Or that you could feel what I do ...but nevertheless
I will try to explain
With mere human words that restrain
My heart pumps with power
Like it is going to burst forth some superpower
My blood seems to pump with more intensity
Stirring up the propensity
To live life to its fullest magnitude
Wondering around with much gratitude
Wish you could see
How you stir up life in me!
And this new contentment
No room for chaos or resentment
No selfish or dishonest intention
And wait did I mention
Never have I experienced this before
And I don't know what that means or what's in store
But that's okay
I just wanted to somehow say
This unexplainable thing inside
Something beautiful rare....I don't want to hide

He loves me

He sees things in me
Thoughts and ways that keep me from being free
I wonder will he love me with all these deficits
Or will I always feel like I belong with the rejected misfits
Wandering about this life
Looking for acceptance only to find pain and strife
He engages in my self-exploration
I become consumed with deep adoration
But now a sudden twist?
My heart begins to race and my eyes mist
Then a calmness reassured
While my history speaks to what I have endured
A love for him has begun
I am comforted knowing true love won't run
So time will tell what this will be
For now I will keep discovering me
If he stays or if he goes
There are a few things I know
To open my heart to loves possibilities
While healing from past travesties
To be true to who I am
And everything doesn't end in a sham!
I have learned that life is give and take
And I must open myself up if good friends are what I want
to make
You have opened my eyes to things that are new
That will forever change what I do
For today I won't worry if you could love me too
I am sure time will show me what to do

Consumed

Drowning in love
Consumed by its intoxication
Basking in its glow
Pumping through my veins
Makes my toes wiggle and feet dance
Makes my thick thighs and curves sexy
Twist in my hips as I walk
Shoulders back
Chest confidently out
Head held high love
Arms sway freely
Heart pumps intensely
Air fills my lungs
My breathe is deep in and out
Mind clear
Gaze is sure and piercing
Words come forth strong and true
Spirit alive
Leaping within
Senses heightened
Love is consuming me now

Spiritual

Created

Life You have created in me
Sinner saved by Grace set free
To Your family I was adopted and entered
Still here on Earth I struggled with being self-centered
I seem to get caught up in life ...distracted
Only to realize it may have been days since we interacted
Father please forgive me for all I do
I know I am nothing without You
My flesh has cravings and it is weak
My spirit is alive and for You it seeks
I seem to drift at times and go astray
You never let me go I'm anchored with You destined to
stay
I know you are always watching looking down
Keeping me from deep waters so I don't drown
When I look in the mirror my imperfections are clear
Body mind and soul alone I have much to fear
But if I imagine myself at Your feet!
You n the throne is where we will meet
Tears falling down my face
God I never want to leave this place
With you strong arms and hands You reach for me
I have dreamt of this I have longed to be
You holding me in the cradle of Your arm
Head on Your chest relieved no more pain or harm
As my tears begin to clear
I'm consumed with love no more fear
A smile comes across my face
No more sin not a trace
I look to Your right hand
Where the Word says He will stand

Face to face with the One who died for me
Who covered my sin set me free
My savior my brother my heart overflows
No words needed just a look He already knows
He reaches out His wounded hand
We embrace now in His physical presence I stand
No longer searching no longer do I roam
Finally I have made it home

Let Go

Let go of the past
Or its painful grip will last
Look back only for the truth you can find
For a short while or to it you will bind
Forgive understand and make amends where you can
Then move on no need to look at it again
Let it go and live in the present
Free yourself from any resentment
Love like it's your first
For Peace and good hunger and thirst
Talk to the Creator throughout your day
Listen and watch for what He will say
Lay your fears and hurts at his feet
And in His presence regularly retreat
Trust that He knows and has something better
This is my letter
To remind me to let go of the past
So its painful grip won't last
To look around at what I have today
It's much greater than my yesterday!

He is there

All along He has been quietly there
All along I have been in His watchful care
In my mother's womb marked with purpose
I plan for me even when I was formless
Injecting poison in their veins did they think of me?
You did ...You designed a future a destiny
Home was not a safe place
But you covered me and knew what I could face
You intentionally placed me in a new environment
This would lay a foundations and give me many a testament
The swing is where I found my peace
Something about the wind a sense of release
My window at sunset is where I talked to You
Crying out for understanding, for family, and what to do
Seems like it took years for me to stop praying that prayer
I always thought you heard me and were right there
All of the pain and rejection
The lies and distorted reflection
You saw and stood by I believe
Not bringing me out You had something greater to achieve
So here I am today
In your Devine presence I have always stayed
You let me know and experience just enough
You know how full life can be and how rough
The Master Craftsman You take your time
Always working, through each valley and climb

Flow Like Water

Someday I'm going to flow like water
My spirit high in the ever after
My mind free of clutter
My mouth it will not utter
Cries of sorrow and desperation
Now singing praises of elevation
To the Most High who claimed my soul
To the One True God who has made me whole
My heart will beat with intensity
Overflowing with joy is what I'll be
Life's cares and problems are all left behind
My scars all healed no longer to remind
Someday I'm going to flow like water
My spirit high in the ever after

Hey-

I want the peace the preacher was talking about today
The kind of peace that lasts and doesn't go away
I want to know You won't give up on me
And that letting go is truly how to be free
I want to know that these dreams are placed by You
I want to know that they will come true!
I want to know I'm on the right track and the purpose in
my life
And at some point will there be any less strife
I want to have that peace that heals
That peace that resonates in day to day deals
That peace that will whisper in my ear
It won't always be like this and dry my tear
The peace that replaces my doubt
What if? When? Why? Maybe I should have went another
route
A peace that consumes my fear
Over my children I love so dear
Peace that will calm this wanting heart
Knowing its desires You placed from the start
A peace that will give me direction
When I'm wondering, sometimes with narrow reflection
Peace over the past hurts choices and mistakes
Peace over the present heart aches
Peace over the future unknowns
Fruit of peace maybe from the seeds that have already
been sown
I want the peace the preacher was talking about today
Kind of peace that lasts and doesn't go away

Shifted

Something has shifted
Out of this mortal body I want to be lifted
Never before has this feeling been so strong
Home home is where I belong
When is it my turn
Oh how this desire burns!
Where are my ruby slippers!
Let me wish on a star the big and little dippers
Make my wish and blow the flame out
Climb to the highest peak and shout!
Take me home! Please! Take me home!
No more is it here I want to roam!
This place is filled with disappointment and pains
My joy peace hope and laughter it drains
I long to feel the comfort of your arms
No more fear no more harms
I'm begging You stating my plea
Home home is where I want to be
The more I know You
The more this is true
This place is filled with hurt and hate
Deception and pride I know You see it this isn't a debate
I'm not denying my part I mean I've participated
But longing for what this world offers has ended
Let me just complete what You sent me here for
And when it's time I will run through that door

Afflicted

In the beginning my presence insignificant
But not to my Creator most Magnificent
My design intentional
His ways unconventional
Born into poverty and addiction
He saw He knew my affliction
Saving my life even at birth
A purpose for me here on earth
Rejection abandonment and pain
Abuse and confusion remain
Somehow he would take all these tragedies
To strengthen me mold me and give me remedies
To heal my heart mind and soul
Wholeness became my goal
Moments of growth and healing
Spiritual insights and feeling my feelings
Yet times of grief and fear
Not trusting anyone and shedding tears
You watch as you have seen this before
This anguish is deep I don't want to feel anymore
And here I am on Sunday afternoon
Needing clarity and breakthrough soon
It's clear what You have done for me already
You have never left stayed with me steady
As I fall short doubt and do my own thing
Your grace and mercy I will cling

Resurrection

We know the story we are told every year
About His purpose please listen with your hearts and hear
A King born in a manager to a carpenter & peasant
He rightfully deserved something much more pleasant
Before His birth his life was at stake
And for my life His they would take
God in human form we are told
Stories of His love never old
The Word living what he would teach
Traveling to places others would not preach
The message of healing and restoration
So worthy of all exhortation
A true Savior humble and all love
Given all power from the Father above
Showing mercy and grace
Even to those who sat in His face
The ultimate sacrifice
Only His body and blood would suffice
So as His friends ran in fear
His mother watched with anguish and tears
As they beat his body and pierced his side
Mocking Him with no place to hide
Father forgive them they know not what they do is what
He would say
Please can't you see He gave His life for you on that day!
No deed can we do to earn
The Saviors ways are what we need learn
The great Redeemer who endured much affliction
Remember today His life, death, and resurrection

The Power

I know I need it ever second, minute, and hour
In Him my life is sustained
His goodness can't be contained
My mind can't fathom His love for me
His grace and mercy sets me free
He is my Creator and Deliverer
The Author and Finisher
He has a perfect plan and purpose for us
We have no reason to doubt or discuss
He knows the desire of our heart
His goodness is what He wants to impart
The bible is full of stories like ours
Women being chosen changed filled with His power
Rahab the prostitute
Living a life that was destitute
Or Mary His faithful mother
Young and poor chosen by the Father
Esther whose people were set to be wiped out
The power gave her another route
Eve whose choice changed the course of humanity
Found forgiveness and kept her spirituality
We share these stories maybe with Leah or Tamar
The woman with the issue of blood, Anna Gomer or Hagar
I don't think we ever expected this baby born in a manger
Would be such a life changer
I think we still struggle to fully comprehend the price
Of His life obedience His sacrifice
He is my El-Roi
In my mother's womb watching over me

Elohim my strength and power
He is my refuge and Hightower
He is my life truth and way
His name is great! He is Yahweh!
All Sufficient One the Great I Am Jehovah Jirah
Elohay Yishi El Rohi Jehovah Rapha
Messiah Vine King Truth El Shaddai
Purifier Great Shepard Comforter Adonai
He is Alpha and Omega the beginning and the end
His ways are so great we cannot comprehend
He is my Abba my protector my heart changer
Keeping me through life's storms and danger
My hope when hopelessness consumes
For in Your house for me You have made room
My light in my darkest moment
Your love leaves me in awe and wonderment
He is my peace He has never left me
Staying by my side despite how I be
His plans for me are great
Even though I can't see my fate
I'm trusting in what only the power can do
Lord God I need You
Praising Him for His goodness shouting His name
Just one touch and you won't be the same
The Power
I know I need it every second minute and hour

Trust Him

Waiting for that booming voice
Either trust Him or not it's my choice
Your heart I have never broken
Shaming words never spoken
Life I gave you at birth
My peace I have for you on earth
You have to trust me with your life
I will see you through all its strife
I know you are hurt and see your tears
I know your desires and your fears
I see your areas of needed growth
But to you My child I gave an oath
Not one familiar to you
This one binding forever true
To never leave or forsake
Never would I consider you a mistake
For your life a purpose and plan
You have to trust I Am the Great I Am
Alpha and Omega is my name
Never changing always the same
So get up and call on me
I am waiting can't you see
For a relationship so binding
What you have been looking for you will be finding
Praise me for who I Am not what I do
Because my child that's why I love you!

Creation

Could the Creator reject His creation?
I mean take a look at our nation
We lack justice and morals
No respect living like immortals
Our nature is corrupt and always wanting more
His grace and mercy we ignore
We break promises and don't follow through
Life is good and we forget about you
We have all the answers and want control
Living our life...bringing death to our soul
The preacher talks about unconditional love
This we don't know much of
So I look up these words unfamiliar
This understanding of love ....so peculiar
What does it mean to be loved this way?
What does it look like how does it feel please convey
Love is defined in numerous ways
I need something simple that I can hold always
Honor, fondness, value, and adoration
Delight, approval, wonder, and affection
Marvel, prize, honor
Pleasure, esteem, and favor
Opposite of these is disgust and hate
Disapproval, contempt...to these I relate
Don't forget about the word unconditional
Because I think it means loving is not optional
Definite, complete, and assured
Genuine, certain, unreserved
It's whole, wide, and unlimited
No strings, outright, unrestricted
It's final, entire, and unquestionable
No fine print, no catch, unmistakable
My Creator..... No more guilt no more shame
He is unconditional love and knows my name

Worth

I try to find you...I seek you diligently
Yet I am at unrest
My mind is frantic, my thoughts race with questions and
what if's
I look for you in achievements
I try to find you in laughter
With unobtainable perfection over and over I fail
I seek you through pleasure
Mere attempts to please through taste and touch
Hiding behind a wall that blocks me from what I seek
Conforming and transforming
Forever changing I search for you
Worth where can I find you
Not in success or failure
Not in shape or size
Not in color or ethnicity
Not in status or accolades
Not in gender or orientation
Not in homes or cars
Not in career or in salary
Not in people or passions
Worth where can I find you
As my wall comes down and I begin to see the beauty of
my smile the glow in my eyes the curves and freckle
spotted skin as I breathe in and feel my lungs fill with life
I feel my heart pound in my chest
As it begins to race I find my worth
I come to the awareness I have been perfectly,
intentionally, and wonderfully made with thought and
purpose
In my Creators hands I find my worth

Fear

I would be lying if I denied
How this fear is creeping back inside
I am sure this is just another level of healing
And maybe for a lifetime I will be dealing
This pain only subsides with a touch
And it's yours I long for so much
It's you my heart is open too
Holding me is just not something you do
So my heart wanders
And my mind wonders
Many men would hold and caress
leave me settling for less
My body longs to be held by strength
Arms of safety at any length
A chest to lean
And stability to glean
My soul yearns for this the most
Actually not me... The Holy Ghost
My body longs for earthly emptiness
But His Spirit resides in me yearning for the Eternal
Greatness
When I focus on what I can touch, heat, taste, and see
I come up short, hurt, and empty
Even now reminded connection to You is Key

Wounded

The wounds are so deep
I just can't keep
Trying to hide the affects
Before anyone inspects
God come in with your healing power
I need it now right this hour!
I know you're working on my heart
And I don't always do my part
Please forgive my humanity
I know it looks and feels like insanity
I have tried to do this by myself
Often putting you on a shelf
Trying to figure all of this out
Progression and regression make me want to shout

Let Go

Let go of the past
Or its painful grip will last
Look back only for the truth you can find
For a short while or to it you will bind
Forgive understand and make amends where you can
Then move on no need to look at it again
Let it go and live in the present
Free yourself from any resentment
Love like it's your first
For Peace and good hunger and thirst
Talk to the Creator throughout your day
Listen and watch for what He will say
Lay your fears and hurts at his feet
And in His presence regularly retreat
Trust that He knows and has something better
This is my letter
To remind me to let go of the past
So its painful grip won't last
To look around at what I have today
It's much greater than my yesterday!

Mold

The mold is being broken
With every word he has spoken
His being shows clear the cracks
Of the strength the mold lacks
A protective outer shell
Keeping me in my own hell
I fight the urge to run
Hi smile like the morning sun
Drawing me to his heart
Oh God break this mold apart
Show me my true being
No longer through this darkens will I be seeing
Who I am and my true reflection
Now it's clear give me time for inspection
So tender is my begin to touch
Shedding this mold I realize I have missed so much
Sensitive to all that surrounds me
So alive I see so clearly
A new birth a new chance
Free to love and free to dance
No mold holding me in or holding me back

Conversations with Him

I want to trust you so much that fear and anxieties no longer exist
I want to trust you so greatly that I can stand firmly upright with confidence
I want to trust you so I walk, talk, and live in boldness
I want to trust You so much that fear does not exist
I want to trust You so much that in the face of pain and adversity I can genuinely smile
I want to trust You so much that I would be a vessel for you and an Oasis for others
I want to trust You so deeply that nothing could shake me
I want to trust You so much that that whatever or whoever is taken away I won't break
I want to trust You so much that when you say go I move
I want to trust You so much that the future and vision for my life is found when I seek You
Whatever hinders me from trusting You fully remove it
You have no need to prove Yourself to me...not anymore
I know who you are God, You are the Healer, Your are the Life Restorer, Sustainer, Father to the fatherless, You are love, You are the Comforter, You are Righteous, Holy, and Good. You are the Author and Finisher, You are God, Creator, Deliver, You are Sovereign. You are detailed and intentional, You are aware and present, You care, You are jealous, You see, You hear, You mourn for us, You are available, You are constant, You are never failing, You are my Helper, Counselor, You all wise, merciful, and full of grace. You are Great!

God says...
I want you to trust Me so much that fear and anxieties no longer exist
I want you to trust Me so greatly that you stand firmly upright with confidence
I want you to trust Me so much that you walk, talk, and live in boldness
I want you to trust Me so much that fear does not exist
I want you to trust Me so much that in the face of pain and adversity you can genuinely smile
I want you to trust Me so much that you would be My vessel and an Oasis for others
I want you to trust Me so deeply that nothing shakes you
I want you to trust Me so much that that whatever or whoever is taken away you won't break
I want you to trust Me so much that when I say go you move
I want you to trust Me so much that the future and vision for your life is found when you seek Me
Whatever hinders you from trusting Me fully remove it, Let it go
I have no need to prove Myself to you...not anymore
You know who I AM, your Healer, your Life Restorer, Sustainer, Father to the fatherless, Unconditional Love, I am your Comforter, I am Righteous, Holy, and Good. I am the Author and Finisher, I am God, Creator, Deliver, Sovereign. I AM detailed and intentional, I AM aware and present, I care, I am jealous,
I see, I hear, I mourn for you, I am available, I am constant, I am Truth, I am Faithful, I am never failing, I am your Helper, Counselor, I am all wise, merciful, and full of grace.

Randoms

Writings

I love it when my pen
Touches the paper and then
dreams feelings pain and memories
Begin to pour out like elixir...sweet remedies
No this isn't something I conjured
Feels like something in me has been punctured
What comes out is so freeing and peaceful
I can't explain it but I'm grateful
Reminds me of the well that won't run dry
The one that is promised to fully satisfy
No longer have to look for peace outside of me
I already have what I need to be free
My faith and this writing
No more internal fighting

Sometimes

Sometimes these writings contain so much hate
keep my pen moving and up late
then there are the other extremes
when my being is filled love hope and dreams
back and forth this pendulum flows
writing things no one knows
unspoken words buried pain
lingering memories and broken promises that remain
a safe refuge a sweet release
A flood gate opened a purging an increase
so much within
not sure where to begin
I have never really had to bring it out
seems as though life itself triggers and bring it about
I just need to pay close attention
to feel what I feel and don't question
just pick up my pen and let the writing express
whatever is deep down whatever has been suppressed

Rain

Its rainy today
So of course the skies are gray
Woke up to the rumbling of thunder
And for some reason filled me with wonder
Never comfort in a storm
Today something different out of the norm
Seems like joy filled the gray sky
And the rain please don't say goodbye
Some sort of new tranquility
A sense of peace coming over me
A smile covers my face
No sign of a dark day not a trace
Not in my universe
Alive is what I'm feeling let me immerse
Myself in the gray, rain, and thunder
Just being....letting my mind wander

Shame

A shame that binds
So many women it finds
Words of how we should be
Daily visuals of the ideal I see
Numbers on the scale to dictate
Only causing self-hate
Sizes defining what's sexy
36 34 36 oh and don't forget a cup C
My nose to pointy or to wide
Oh and that gut please hide
Legs so short or to long
Never ok always something wrong
Skin to dark to white to caramel
Don't forget the concealer girl you look like hell
Told we should look like this or that
Always the message ...you're too thin too fat
I say we begin to embrace ourselves
That we put the quick fixes and pills back on the shelves
If we could see the beauty that flows from deep within
Girl your creation you were created to win
Love your legs your hips all those curves and that beautiful face
No longer have competing and comparing just begun to embrace
Your thin straight or curly hair
Your breasts, waist, hips, I don't care
Love your body your shape your size
Please no longer compromise
The beauty that is specific to you
A princess a queen you are so be true!

Silence

Silence is what I need
To my heart and feelings I must heed
Crazy how what I use to fear
Now has so much value and dear
Think of all these years of holding this in
Wanting these feelings to come up I can't imagine
Never before was it like this
All this verbal beauty coming surface
Taught to suppress and hide
Trust no one and never confide
Fears wonders dreams and passions
I'm telling you about other oppressions
More than what our naked eye can see
More than ethnicity and poverty
These are certainly forms
That have been accepted as societal norms
Crippling and devastating if we let them be
But I want to fight and learn how to be free
So I write with no fear or limitation
The truth for me no alteration
Offending some and giving words to others
Healing and freedom for my sisters and brothers
A gift I have finally accepted
So unexpected
May be from my life there will be a line or verse
I don't think it matters that our stories are diverse

As humans there are things I know we share
Poor or rich educated or not I don't care
We all have desires goals feelings dreams
Anything can happen and rip them at the seams
Causing us to fear and doubt
Praying God give us another route
I hope you hear what I'm trying to say
There is an oppression that leads you away
Forcing you to deny yourself and conform to expectations
Another human being setting limitations
This is no joke or just another rhyme
Our culture and society does it all the time
Fitting a cookie cutter mold of what we should be
Labels and judgment when we don't fit agree?!
Tired of living within boundaries
Our own personal penitentiaries
Whether bound by lies you have been told
When you were young and now old
It's never too late to discover
The truth about yourself and recover
We all have scars
We all have a destiny a future all created to shine like stars
I encourage you to free yourself to be true
And share that gift that is within you

Sleepless nights

I wonder where these sleepless nights come from
They aren't every night just some
Makes me wonder if they have meaning or purpose
Frustrated I haven't taken the time to question or focus
Is there a message my Creator is trying to get through
Here I am Lord speak! Tell me what to do!
If I could sleep through just one night
I mean straight through eyes closed tight
A deep deep sleep
With sweet dreams no counting sheep
I wonder how that would be
Waking up ready to go energy
But no here I am turning and tossing
Thoughts in my mind crossing
My dreams waiting to be dreamed
I JUST WANT TO SLEEP I screamed
3:30 in the am I'm getting a little tired now
Eyelids heavy maybe this writing will allow
A couple more hours of sleep
No more tossing and turning not a peep
Wish me luck
In my bed I am tucked!

My Day

I'm so tired it's the end of my day
Not enough energy to play
Always enough to write down these ideas though
They seem to come with little effort they just flow
I wonder when the writing will change
So many things to write I think it is strange
My kids, my God, recovery
Life experiences and self-discovery
Right now just love fears and childhood
I would like to say I'm all good
But that would be deception
Going through a process trying to change my perception
On what my life has been
Not sure I want to do it again
So my story I am reflecting
My experiences I am respecting
Each one for a reason a purpose
Maybe just for now so I can right these verses
Revealing hurts and trauma
Trying to release what's inside no more drama
Letting go from the past the binds
Maybe helping others clear their minds
No longer holding this pain within
I'm getting stronger from the past I will win

Awake

Laying here wide awake
I'm tired but mind just won't shake
Thoughts starting to go
Eyes wide open words beginning to flow
I fight it I want to go to sleep
But I'm curious I want to see what will come out so I keep
My fingers tips ready
Typing these phrases steady
It's like a bottle shaken with all this pressure
The only relief is to write gives me much pleasure
The feeling when the writing is complete
Not sure if you understand but nothing competes
Like nothing I ever experienced before
God only knows what's in store!

Numb

My body is numb
My hands my lips
My hearts not heavy
But there is a little sickness I feel In the pit of my stomach
Life is good I mean real good
And I feel like escaping
Vanishing In the clouds
Melting in the rain drops
Slowly gracefully taken with the wind
Or consumed by the earth
No particular thing has occurred
But I feel the frustration of something
It's pushing on the forefront of my skull
As I attempt to walk this out
The air breathes on my face
The clouds of the storm begin to cover me
While the night comes
Lingering piercing through is the sunset and what's left of
the blue sky
The rain is coming
It's trapped in the atmosphere but u can feel it
You can smell it
My tears are trapped
They usually flow so naturally
So easily
But not today I can feel them like the rain in the
atmosphere
And like the rain and storm they will come
Like the rain and storm they come to an end
The sky will be bluer the grass greener and the air fresher

Digest and Purge

I can no longer digest these words
So on this paper I do purge
The words and ideas
Memories and Pains
Of my childhood I do start
I remember us always apart
I do not know a comforting touch
Something I longed from you very much
Your hand on my head pressing to your chest
Holding me tight praying you did your best
Tears flowing down my face
But peace resides because I know I found my place
Of your love I do wonder....

Get Lost

I want to get lost in the paper
Hide in the colors
Blend in with the shades
I want to get lost in the paper
Where anything is created No rules or wrongs
Just freedom and beauty
I want to get lost in the paper
Where the creation is and spectators linger
Where individuality is embraces and common things are
not common
I want to get lost in the paper
Where passions are placed
Where dreams and visions are recorded
Where stories begin and end
I want to get lost in the paper

What is slavery?

Is it limited to a certain place and time?
Names replaced and value decreased to a dime
Is slavery solely defined for those ripped from their
families?
Stripped from their culture and countries?
For those that were treated less than humane
Only the most resilient would remain
To those who have been beaten and brutalized
Those that the white man capitalized
For those forced to learn a new language
Forced to forget their culture and heritage?
Young girls and women forced to succumb to their owners
desires
Being sold over and over to the highest buyers
Men beaten bloody and hung
Spread fear in the rest old and young
A continuous raping of relationships and identity
Raping of dignity and worth a nonentity
Children and churches burned
Nothing for tem could be earned
Now we have a group of poets, writers, and activists
Challenging mainstream a group of nonconformists
Powerful writers and orators
Independent thinkers and passionate educators
A group that detest slavery and everything is stood for
Who demand the truth and determined to get more
Who refer to their females counterparts as Queen
And he her King a mutual respect between
I am saying all of this to lay a foundation
We have now ongoing levels of degradation
Present day slavery
Stealing our children, men, and women, thievery
Stripping their identity for a price
And what they give and receive will never suffice
No no need to reach back to Jamestown Virginia

We can start with our children and the pedophilia
How they are made slaves to perversion and secrets
Forgive me this is just how my brain interprets
A culture that breeds sex sells
1619 or 2015 it enslaves compels
Young boys to find status in their conquers
Culture not cultivating free thinkers
Enslaved to sex and the streets
Making rhymes about dope and money lame beats
Talents and gifts reduced to crime and pulling triggers
No no need to reach back
Look at our boys and young men you can see the lack
We have a world where sex sells
For many women survival and money compels
Others have bought into the slave mind
Professing their good don't knock my grind
As they allow themselves to be misused
Many just reliving their childhood being abused
Spreading their legs for money
The people cheer "Shake that ass dot it honey!"
Slavery has not ended I am telling you!
It has only evolved...it's the acceptable thing to do
We prepare our girls for their sexualized future
TV, Media, lack of nurture
And if their beauty isn't the current trend
We've got surgeries and waste trimmers to bend
In just the right places, lashes, and extensions
Pills and lifts to get the right dimensions
Slavery isn't limited to history
Our identities continue to be a mystery
Selling ourselves into slavery continuously
Its influence affecting each generation continually
Slavery has never ended it has evolved
We need to get in the now... get involved

Human Disorder

Peace for pleasure
Truth for deception
Joy for a high
Integrity for bad character
Love for lust
Friendships for Pharisees
Quality for instant gratification
Humanness for zombie state
Life for death
Serenity for chaos
Foundation for destruction
Faith for self
Gratitude for emptiness
Living for survival
Freedom for bondage
Wholeness for brokenness
Healing for wounded
Royalty for rags
Wisdom for foolishness

Richness for depravity
Hope for hopelessness
Worth for shame
Fullness for never ending emptiness
Self-love for self-hate
Humility for self-righteousness
Belonging for isolation
Dreams for today
Spirituality for spiritual depravity
Boundaries for invasion
Overcomer for victim
Child of God for an orphan
Purpose for lack of worth
Direction for wandering
Clarity for confusion
Forgiveness for resentments
Value for worthlessness

Dandelions

Lord I want to be like a dandelion
Bright full yellow flower bursting forth from a weed.
Yes! This is what I want to be indeed
Their soft petals like velvet
Rub them in your cheeks, they will turn yellow I bet
Dandelions are resilient and strong
Some are short and some are long
Plucked and put together a crown!
Always beautiful in our hair golden brown
We would tuck them behind our ear
Yep this is what we did every year
They were beautiful in our green lawn
A yellow blanket they seemed to belong
Some were puffy white
Littlest of wind and its seeds took flight
Going wherever the wind would carry
Where ever they landed they would bury
A plant so persistent and resilient
Producing a flower so bright and brilliant
A flower so delicate and whimsical
I know this may sound a little fanatical
But there is a joy and beauty from this unwanted thing.
Their arms spread fists filled in the spring
Puffy white things floating through the air
No control landing where they may and don't care
Lord I want to be like a dandelion
Bright full yellow flower bursting forth from a weed
Yes this is what I want to be indeed

Life and Death

We know that in life a few things are sure
Life and death both have challenges and hard to endure
Life a twisted rollercoaster
It can have you so high! But you best not boaster
What goes up must come down
Life will smack that grin to a frown
Let me tell you like this
Life can have you high like that first kiss
Then throw you a curve ball
When you realize love doesn't love you at all
Or how about that new job... more money!
Still can't get ahead got you feeling crummy
For every joy there seems to be a sorrow
Have hope but still wonder about tomorrow
Faith is challenged on every side
Better buckle up and hold on for the ride
Do I even need to mention putting our loved ones to rest
A time of mourning but still have to put on Sundays best
We believe in a life lived happily in the ever after
The good life no tears or sickness with the Master
A time that is so bitter sweet
A loss a pain that knocks us off our feet
No words can bring comfort
People try with food scripture ....all their effort
Nothing but time will dull the pain
We will get up and our strength regain
A mixture of mourning and rejoice
If we could just one more time hear their voice
Only in our night dreams and sometimes our day
Will we have sweet visions and remember what they
would say
We know that in life a few things are sure
Life and death both have challenges and hard to endure

Beat of the Drum

Listening to the beat of the drum
Listening to the music you make ...I succumb
To the rhythm my heart begins to beat
No longer do I want to retreat
Alive I begin to feel
This peace coming over me surreal
As I close my eyes and feel the sound
I wish no one was around
So I could close my eyes and go to another place
In the long grass with the wind on my face
Spread on the ground with my arms open wide
Open and free nothing to hide
The willow trees limbs blowing softly in the breeze
The sound of the stream putting my heart at ease
Breathing the fresh air breathing deep
Releasing those things I don't want to keep
Pains and worries of this life
Living being...no strife
Connected to the world connected to my being
This music you make so freeing

A night of release

Words a flirtatious tease
If I close my eyes and listen to your voice
Getting lost in your painted words would be my choice
It's not just the words alone
It's the dreams and ideas that have been sown
Your body in response to what flows
The rhythm in your speech everyone knows
A piece of you has been purged
Now meaning and purpose has emerged
I want to live more
My life is where my words are store

Humans

Relationships with humans are too much
But I don't want to be alone so to them I clutch
It doesn't matter how 'good' that person maybe
Hurt will come it's a guarantee
It doesn't matter your position in life
Father son sister or wife
Counselor, mother, or teacher
Police officer, doctor, or preacher
Encourager's protectors and providers
Healers and life guiders
All marred and imperfect
Causing pain and neglect
If this is a given a promise to happen
Do we just accept it and move on with no hesitation
How do you not let the words actions penetrate your heart?
How do you hold it together and not fall apart
Is there a way to desensitize?
Without compromise?
Is there a way to love carefully?
Without being vulnerable to the inevitable truly?
I am confused our heart can't avoid being bruised

Help

I asked for help today
Really looking for a quick easy way
To rid myself if this brain that just won't stop
And get some sleep before I completely drop
You see life can get pretty intense
I get overwhelmed and feel I have no defense
I mean you feel like everything is on you
Provision future responsibilities survival what to do
So you carefully build a wall of protection
Wouldn't believe what u saw if you did an inspection
This is what I must hide
Can't trust no one to confide
Sometimes we just have to allow time to do its part
When it comes to matters of the heart
Truth it will unfold
If its love they do hold
So just be patient and wait
And soon enough you will know your fate
If this was meant for a season
Or a deeper greater reason
In the meantime learn what you must
And in time do put your trust

Dedication

This book of poems is dedicated to all of the children that have a story and no voice, to all those teenagers who have been labeled and misunderstood, and to all of the adults who are hiding their hurt and pain behind some dysfunction.

I would like to thank my God who gave me these experiences and also a way out to heal. I also will be forever thankful for Amefika Terrell for stirring this gift up in me and encouraging me to continue along the way. Forever thankful! I also want to thank my friends and family that supported me as well.

About the Author

My name is Georgia Caldwell, I was born and raised in Minnesota. My writings have been outpourings from my innermost and have been an amazing source of healing. I hope that my writings can give others a voice as well.

www.ingramcontent.com/pod-product-compliance
Lightning Source LLC
Chambersburg PA
CBHW032040040426
42449CB00007B/960